ACCA

Paper F7 (INT)

Financial reporting

Pocket notes

ACCA
Approved Publisher

KAPLAN
PUBLISHING

British library cataloguing-in-publication data

A catalogue record for this book is available from the British Library.

Published by:
Kaplan Publishing UK
Unit 2 The Business Centre
Molly Millars Lane
Wokingham
Berkshire
RG41 2QZ

978-1-84710-306-2

© FTC Kaplan Limited, 2007
Printed and bound in Great Britain by
William Clowes Ltd, Beccles, Suffolk

Contents

KAPLAN PUBLISHING

The exam

The exam is a three-hour paper (plus 15 minutes reading time) structured as follows:

		Number of marks
Question 1	Preparation of group financial statements, possibly including a "small" discussion element	25
Question 2	Reporting of non-group financial statements	25
Question 3	Appraisal of performance, possibly involving cash flow statements	25
Questions 4 and 5	These questions will cover the remainder of the syllabus and will be worth 15 and 10 marks respectively	25
		100

All questions are **compulsory**.

The mechanical aspects of question 1's group accounts can be mastered through practice. The most important thing is to attempt as many questions as possible, ideally under simulated exam conditions. It is important to take time to understand the processes involved in preparing the figures so that you can deal with any unexpected adjustments that the examiner might introduce and also so that you can deal with any narrative parts to question 1.

Question 2 might involve preparing a set of accounts in the IAS 1 format. If so, it could include 5 or 6 detailed adjustments in respect of accounting standards. Alternatively, it could involve revising a set of draft financial statements. The adjustments require a broad knowledge of the syllabus. Again, the key is to practice.

Question 3 could combine ratio analysis with the interpretation of a cash flow statement. The key to any performance appraisal question at this level is to have some appreciation of business. Reading the financial press (either newspapers and magazines or online) will help you to understand business.

Questions 4 and 5 can be on any part of the syllabus and are there to test your knowledge in more detail. Read each question carefully, identify exactly what the question is asking you to do, and then plan your answer observing strict time control.

Make sure that you provide neat and tidy workings whenever a question involves computation. These will enable the marker to give you due credit if you make an error in one part of your answer. It will also encourage you to work in a logical and methodical way, saving you time and reducing the likelihood of making mistakes.

Revision

- Practice consolidations and accounts preparation until you can do it quickly and accurately without fail; you will then have the means to score up to 50 marks in the exam.

- Use these Pocket Notes to give yourself a broad and thorough knowledge and understanding of the whole syllabus; this will ensure that you have the ability to score well on the other questions.

- Supplement text and study material with a good understanding of business. Reflect on any practical experience that you have. Read as widely as you can, bearing in mind that many good newspapers and business magazines have web pages that can be browsed free of charge.

- In the exam, make sure you attempt 4 questions. This is a very time pressured exam and you may need to leave a question unfinished and move on in order to do this. Many students fail each year because they only complete 3 questions and it wasn't enough to gain a pass.

1

Regulatory framework

In this chapter

- The standard setting system.
- The regulatory framework.
- Principles-based v rules based accounting.
- Not-for-profit and public sector entities.

The standard setting system

Accounting standards are necessary in order to enable companies to produce financial statements that are relatively consistent. This makes it easier for readers to understand and interpret their companies' accounts.

Accounting standards are set by the accountancy profession. The most important aspect of the standard setting process occurs at the international level.

The most important body for our purposes is the International Accounting Standards Board (IASB).

The IASC Foundation
Responsible for governance of the standard setting process.

IASB
Responsible for setting accounting standards (IFRSs).

SAC
Forum for experts from different countries and different business sectors to offer advice to IASB.

IFRIC
Issues rapid guidance on accounting matters where divergent interpretations of IFRSs have arisen.

Accounting standards

The IASB sets standards in the form of International Financial Reporting Standards (IFRSs).

The IASB inherited a number of International Accounting Standards (IASs) from its predecessor body.

The International Financial Reporting Interpretations Committee (IFRIC) deals with loopholes that arise in existing standards.

Exam focus

Most IFRSs and IASs are examinable in this paper.

The IFRIC pronouncements are not examinable.

The standards generally do not have any direct legal status. In most countries it is a legal requirement that financial statements 'present fairly' or give a 'true and fair view'.

In practice, the IFRSs, IASs and IFRICs provide a basis for external auditors and other regulators to assess the extent to which the standards comply with these criteria.

Setting standards

Key Point

Standards are set by a process of consultation.

The IASB identifies a subject and establishes an advisory committee to recommend an appropriate treatment.

Each standard is preceded by an exposure draft, which gives the public the opportunity to comment.

At any stage the IASB might issue a discussion paper.

The final version of the IFRS is published provided eight of the 14 members of the IASB agree to do so.

National standard setting bodies

The IASB works in partnership with the major national standard setting bodies.

All the most important national standard setters are represented on the IASB and their views are taken into account so that a consensus can be reached.

The regulatory framework

Users of financial statements must be able to rely on them for decision making purposes. There is a wide range of users who rely heavily on financial statements.

The preparation of accounts for publication is affected by a range of rules and regulations in addition to IFRSs. These include:

- national company law
- EU directives (which provide a framework for company law within the EU)
- stock exchange rules.

Principles-based v rules-based accounting

There is a major debate in the US about the role of rules v principles in accounting regulation.

Principles-based accounting involves preparing financial statements so that they meet a set of principle-based criteria. For example, UK financial statements must give a 'true and fair view'.

Rules-based accounting puts the requirement to comply with each individual accounting standard first. This has been the case, for example, in the US. This approach has been blamed for the problems that arose in the case of Enron, where the auditors knew that the financial statements were potentially misleading, but could do nothing about it because they complied with all the rules.

The main difference between principles-based and rules-based accounting is that the former has a "true and fair override", which means that it is not only possible, but mandatory to ignore the rules if doing so is required in order to avoid producing misleading financial statements.

Not-for-profit and public sector entities

The corporate objectives of businesses are very different from those of not-for-profit and public sector entities.

Companies exist largely to make profits. They have a range of stakeholders, the most important of whom is generally the body of shareholders. Financial statements are intended to communicate the profitability and viability of the business.

Not-for-profit and public sector entities do not exist to make profits, but they do have a diverse range of stakeholders, many of whom have a legitimate interest in the body's financial stewardship.

In practice, the accounting policies adopted by not-for-profit and public sector entities are increasingly similar. For example, government bodies generally have to produce the equivalent of an income statement and balance sheet and these are generally prepared in same manner as would be used by a business.

2

A conceptual framework

In this chapter

- What is a conceptual framework?
- Content of the Framework.

What is a conceptual framework?

A conceptual framework is:

- a coherent system of interrelated objectives and fundamental principles
- a framework which prescribes the nature, function and limits of financial accounting and financial statements.

Without a conceptual framework (CF) standard setters will find it difficult to produce accounting standards that are consistent with one another.

Key Point

It is difficult to decide on the most appropriate treatment of a problem issue 'from first principles' unless it is agreed what those principles are.

The IASB has a CF document known as Framework for the Preparation and Presentation of Financial Statements ("Framework"). This document is on the list of IASB publications that is examinable.

The Framework should be the starting point for any IASB working party that has been asked to comment on or make suggestions for any problem that has arisen with existing standards. Amongst other things, it sets out the user groups and their information requirements and proposes in outline how best to satisfy those needs.

Contents of the Framework

Exam focus

You should have a broad understanding of the contents of the Framework. You might have to explain the logic behind an accounting standard and the Framework will provide you with a sound basis for doing so.

The Framework contains the following chapters:

- the objective of financial statements

- underlying assumptions
- qualitative characteristics of financial statements
- the elements of financial statements
- recognition of the elements of financial statements
- concepts of capital and capital maintenance.

The objective of financial statements

Key Point

The objective of financial statements is to provide information about the financial position, performance and changes in financial position of an entity that is useful to a wide range of users in making economic decisions.

In practice, this boils down to providing users with information about the entity's ability to generate cash.

Cash is not the same as profit. However, the income statement provides an indication of the entity's ability to create wealth and, by implication, generate net cash from its operations so that it might pay dividends to its shareholders.

The balance sheet contains a host of non-cash balances. However, the balance sheet does give readers an indication of the capacity to generate cash by giving information about the resources available to the business and the manner in which they have been invested.

Underlying assumptions

Key Point

Financial statements are prepared under the accruals and going concern bases.

Qualitative characteristics of financial statements

Key Point

Qualitative characteristics are the attributes that make the information provided in financial statements useful to users.

Information is useful if it is:

- relevant
- reliable
- comparable
- understandable.

Information can only be useful if it is material. Information is only material if its omission or misstatement could influence the decisions of users.

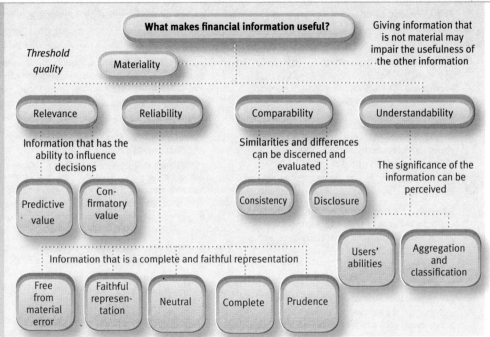

What makes financial information useful?

Giving information that is not material may impair the usefulness of the other information

Threshold quality

Materiality

Relevance

Reliability

Comparability

Understandability

Information that has the ability to influence decisions

Similarities and differences can be discerned and evaluated

The significance of the information can be perceived

Predictive value

Confirmatory value

Consistency

Disclosure

Users' abilities

Aggregation and classification

Information that is a complete and faithful representation

Free from material error

Faithful representation

Neutral

Complete

Prudence

The elements of financial statements

Key Point

The definitions of the elements, particularly of assets and liabilities, are of fundamental importance. They determine the accounting treatment of a host of items in the financial statements.

Everything that is recognised in the financial statements can be classified in terms of one of the five elements as defined below.

Definition

An **asset** is a resource controlled by the entity as a result of past events and from which future economic benefits are expected to flow to the entity.

Note that ownership is not mentioned anywhere in the definition of assets. It is possible to obtain control without ever becoming the owner (e.g. through a lease agreement) and so some of an entity's assets could be owned by someone else.

Definition

A **liability** is a present obligation of the entity arising from past events, the settlement of which is expected to result in an outflow from the entity of resources embodying economic benefits.

Defining liabilities has been a major source of difficulty in the past. Companies have sought to identify ways of raising finance without having to recognise any liability in the balance sheet ('off-balance sheet financing'). This definition could mean that a liability has to be recognised even though the entity does not 'owe' anything.

Key Point

All of the other definitions follow on from those for assets and liabilities.

Definition

Equity is the residual interest in the assets of the entity after deducting all its liabilities.

Assets = Equity + Liabilities
Equity = Assets − Liabilities

Definition

Income is increases in economic benefits during the accounting period in the form of inflows or enhancements of assets or decreases of liabilities that result in increases in equity, other than those relating to contributions from equity participants.

Definition

Expenses are decreases in economic benefits during the accounting period in the form of outflows or depletions of assets or incurrences of liabilities that result in decreases in equity, other than those relating to distributions to equity participants.

Recognition of the elements of financial statements

Items that do not meet the recognition criteria cannot be included in the financial statements.

Key Point

An item can only be recognised in the financial statements if:

- it is probable that any future economic benefit associated with the item will flow to or from the entity; and

- the item has a cost or value that can be measured with reliability.

Thus, an expense would have to meet the definition laid down in the previous section of the Framework and meet these criteria.

Concepts of capital

Generally, the figures in the financial statements are measured at their historical cost or at a valuation. This is probably as much as you need to know about capital measurement. However, the Framework introduces the possibility of alternative approaches.

Under **financial capital maintenance** the company has to allow for the impact of changes to the purchasing power of each unit of currency in arriving at a profit figure.

For example, a bank account containing $1,000 would have bought more at the beginning of the year than it would at the end because of the effects of inflation. Financial capital maintenance would take this loss of purchasing power into account.

Under **physical capital maintenance** the company has to make provision for keeping its physical productive capacity at the same level at the end of the year as at the beginning in calculating profits.

For example, a factory production line will have suffered some wear and tear during the year. Rather than charging depreciation

based on historical cost the company should consider the possibility that the specific cost of replacing the equipment at the end of its life might have risen and this will have to be taken into account in determining profit.

Exam focus

These concepts might be regarded as theoretical for the moment, although the accounting standards relating to fixed assets are increasingly requiring the reporting of values rather than cost less depreciation.

3

Accounting concepts and policies

In this chapter

- IAS 8 Accounting policies, changes in accounting estimates and errors.
- Measurement in financial statements.
- Faithful representation.

IAS 8 accounting policies, changes in accounting estimates and errors

Exam focus

IAS 8 is an important standards because it clarifies the accounting treatment of a variety of accounting issues, including:

- selection of accounting policies
- changes in accounting policies
- changes in accounting estimates
- correction of prior period errors.

Accounting policies

Definition

Accounting policies are the principles, bases, conventions, rules and practices applied by an entity which specify how the effects of transactions and other events are reflected in the financial statements.

IAS 8 requires an enterprise to select and apply appropriate accounting policies complying with International Financial Reporting Standards (IFRSs) and Interpretations to ensure that the financial statements provide information that is:

- relevant to the decision-making needs of users
- reliable in that they:
- represent faithfully the results and financial position of the
- enterprise
- reflect the economic substance of events and transactions and
- not merely the legal form
- are neutral, i.e. free from bias
- are prudent
- are complete in all material respects.

Changes in accounting policies

True changes in accounting policies are very rare. It can be difficult to introduce these into a question. Take care not to treat a simple change in an estimate as a rather more complicated change in accounting policy.

Accounting policies should remain the same from period to period in order to allow for consistency of treatment.

There could be very rare occasions when a change of policy is required (e.g. the existing policy has been superseded by a new IFRS or management has decided that the old policy is no longer appropriate and has to be changed).

In order to preserve the appearance of consistency, a change in accounting policies is accounted for as follows:

- the new policy will be applied retrospectively, with the opening balance on retained earnings recalculated on the basis that the new policy had always been in force

- the resulting change in the retained earnings brought forward will be shown as a prior period adjustment in the statement of changes in equity

- comparatives will be restated as if the new policy had been in force during the previous period.

The change and its effects must be described in the notes to the accounts.

Accounting estimates

Many of the figures in the financial statements rely on estimates.

Inevitably, some estimates will be revised in the light of unfolding events and new information.

Changes in accounting estimates are recognised in the income statement in the same period as the change occurs and included under the same classification as for the original asset.

If the change is material then it should be disclosed in the notes to the financial statements.

Prior period errors

Exam focus

Again, care should be taken to avoid misclassifying a simple change in accounting estimate as something more complicated.

Definition

Prior period errors are omissions from, and misstatements in, the financial statements for one or more prior periods arising from a failure to use information that:

- was available when the financial statements for those periods were authorised for issue and

- could reasonably be expected to have been taken into account in preparing those financial statements.

Prior period errors are dealt with by:

- restating the opening balance of assets, liabilities and equity as if the error had never occurred, and presenting the necessary adjustment to the opening balance of retained earnings in the statement of changes in equity

- restating the comparative figures presented, as if the error had never occurred.

These adjustments should be disclosed in full in the notes to the accounts.

Measurement in financial statements

There are several bases for measuring the figures in financial statements. Some are in common use, while others are of a more theoretical nature.

Historical cost

Assets are valued in the balance sheet at their cost.

Non-current assets are depreciated over time.

Fair value

Fair value is the amount at which an asset or liability could be exchanged in an arm's length transaction between informed and willing parties, other than in a forced or liquidation sale.

Replacement cost

The cost to the business of replacing the asset.

Net realisable value

The estimated sale proceeds less any costs involved in selling the asset.

Economic value

The present value of the future cash flows from an asset.

> **Key Point**

In practice, accounting statements are prepared using a combination of different accounting bases.

In theory, it would be possible to develop a whole system of accounting that used one or other basis exclusively for all assets and liabilities.

For example:

- inventory is valued at the lower of historical cost and net realisable value
- non-current assets are usually valued at either depreciated historical cost or their fair value
- 'impaired' non-current assets are valued at either their economic value or their net realisable value.

Thus, most assets are shown at their historical costs, but some are valued under an alternative basis.

Pure historical cost accounting

Valuing transactions at their historical cost has the advantage of generating figures that are relatively objective and verifiable.

The resulting information produced can be problematic when used for decision-making purposes:

- balance sheet figures can bear very little relevance to any form of economic decisions
- the income statement overstates earnings.

In practice, prices are always changing. Rising prices mean that historical costs quickly become out of date and are useless for decision-making purposes. Price rises also create problems for calculating profit because inventory might be purchased weeks or even months before it is sold. That can mean that something sold for $100 in October is being costed in July $, when prices were lower. This distortion is even worse when depreciation is deducted from revenue, because the depreciation charge is based on asset costs that might be years out of date.

Current purchasing power accounting (CPP)

CPP is a simple method of adjusting for the effects of inflation.

Government bodies keep careful track of the purchasing power of their currency so that they can calculate the rate of inflation.

Their results are expressed in the form of a retail price index.

Key Point

The retail price index is a measure of the relative purchasing power of a unit of currency.

For example, the UK retail price index increased by 4.5% from April 2006 until April 2007. That was measured by taking a basket of goods and measuring their prices as at the beginning and end of the period (in fact, the government checks these prices every month).

The inflation rate is a measure of the extent to which the purchasing power of £1 or $1 has declined. This is, however, a very general measure. It does not mean that every single price has risen by that amount. The specific prices of individual items might have risen (or fallen) by different amounts to give an average increase overall of 4.5%.

CPP accounting recalculates historical cost figures so that they are all stated in consistent $ units. For example, a simple balance sheet might show non-current assets that were bought in December 2003 and July 2005, inventory that was purchased in October 2007 and cash and trade receivables expressed in December 2007 $. The retail price index information published by the government makes it possible to restate all of the figures in terms of December 2007 $.

A CPP balance sheet has the effect of stating equity in terms of the "purchasing power" that the owners' investment had at the year end. This means that the effects of inflation are taken into account in arriving at the owners' return.

CPP is relatively simple to calculate because it starts with historical cost figures and multiplies each one by the appropriate index figures to get to a consistent $ value.

CPP is flawed in the sense that the business is subject to specific price changes that may not be particularly closely approximated by the retail price index. For example, a property company could be faced with a slump in property prices at a time when prices throughout the economy are generally rising.

The best way to imagine CPP equity is to picture it as a financial investment made by the shareholders, ignoring the nature of the business or what it does.

If a business breaks even in terms of CPP accounting then it has maintained the purchasing power of the shareholders' investment.

Replacement cost accounting (RC)

RC is sometimes referred to as Current Cost Accounting (CCA).

Replacement cost accounting adjusts for the effects of specific price changes, rather than the general rate of inflation.

For example, suppose a piece of inventory is sold for $10. Under RC accounting the cost of this inventory will be determined by looking at the cost of replacing the inventory as at the date of sale. If the inventory was purchased for a historical cost of $7 but cost $8 to replace at the time of sale then the RC profit is $2 ($10-$8).

RC accounting also bases the depreciation charge on the cost of replacing non-current assets rather than their historical cost.

Valuing inventory and non-current assets in this way ensures that the business maintains its operating capacity (e.g. if it bakes bread then it will only report a profit after it has provided for the replacement of the non-current assets and inventory consumed during the year's manufacturing).

RC accounting can be complicated and expensive to apply.

Determining the replacement cost of assets and inventory can be simplified by using specialised indices that relate to those assets, but it still requires a great deal of effort.

There can also be theoretical problems. For example, if a company has a Mark 1 production line then should it base its replacement costs on those of similar Mark1 machines when it would be buying a more up-to-date Mark 2 machine if it was forced to make a replacement?

Key Point

The best way to imagine RC equity is to picture the business in terms of its manufacturing capacity.

If a business breaks even in terms of RC accounting then it has maintained the business' manufacturing capacity.

The shareholders might find RC accounting slightly confusing and even slightly irrelevant. Their interest is really in ensuring that the purchasing power of their dividends is maintained from year to year.

Exam focus

RC figures are possibly of more interest to managers rather than to shareholders.

Capital maintenance

Key Point

Profit should not be declared until capital has been maintained, otherwise the company might pay tax and dividends out of capital rather than out of earnings.

Each of the three bases we have looked at has a different concept of capital maintenance.

Historical cost

Capital is measured in terms of the historical cost of net assets.

This has no real economic significance, unless historical costs are a reasonable surrogate for some alternative basis.

This is sometimes known as "money" financial capital maintenance.

CPP

Capital is measured in terms of the owners' purchasing power.

Capital is maintained in financial terms.

RC

Capital is measured in terms of the business' operating capacity.

Capital is maintained in physical terms.

Faithful representation

Financial statements should give a 'faithful representation' or a 'true and fair view'.

Exam focus

There is no adequate definition of the terms 'faithful representation' or 'true and fair'.

In practice, financial statements will be deemed to have achieved these requirements if they:

- conform with accounting standards
- conform with the any relevant legal requirements
- have applied the qualitative characteristics from the Framework.

IAS 1 Presentation of financial statements requires that financial statements that have been prepared in accordance with IFRS should disclose that fact.

In very rare circumstances, it is possible that applying an IFRS or IAS would be misleading in the context of a specific company. On those occasions it is acceptable to implement the '\' and prepare the statements on an alternative basis, which would then have to be justified and explained in the notes to the financial statements.

It is highly unusual for it to be appropriate

to implement the true and fair override.
You should not suggest doing so in the
exam unless the examiner appears to
have exaggerated the circumstances in the
question so that there is really no alternative.

4

Principles of consolidated financial statements

In this chapter

- The concept of group accounts.
- Definition of a subsidiary.

The concept of group accounts

There will be a compulsory group accounts question in the exam.

You will find it much easier if you understand the nature and purpose of group accounts.

A group comprises two or more companies that are controlled as a single economic entity.

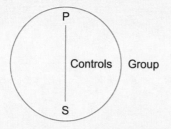

For example, P and S are two separate companies. P owns 100% of the equity of S and, because of this, controls S's activities.

In theory, the investment in S could be P's only asset and dividends received from S could be P's only income. P's shareholders might not find the company's financial statements very interesting because the asset value attributed to S will probably remain at its cost from one year to the next and the dividends received from S might not give much of an insight into S's financial health.

We overcome this problem by preparing a set of financial statements that present P and S as a single economic entity.

Group accounts combine the financial statements of the various group members as present the result as if the separate companies were a single economic entity.

Chapter 4

This is logical because they are, by definition, all under the holding company's control.

Applicable accounting standards

The following standards relate to the preparation of consolidated financial statements:

- IFRS 3 Business combinations
- IAS 27 Consolidated and separate financial statements
- IAS 28 Investments in associates.

Definition of a subsidiary

Both IAS 27 and IFRS define a subsidiary in the same way.

Definition

Subsidiary – an entity that is controlled by another entity (known as the parent)

Control – the power to govern the financial and operating policies of an enterprise so as to obtain benefits from its activities.

Control can be established in a number of ways:

- ownership of more than 50% of voting power
- control of more than half the voting rights by virtue of an agreement with other investors
- the ability to govern the financial and operating policies of the entity under a statute or an agreement
- the right to appoint or remove the majority of the members of the board of directors
- the right to cast the majority of votes at a meeting of the board of directors.

Exam focus

The definition of the holding company/ subsidiary company relationship is complicated because there have been scandals in the past with holding companies attempting to exclude subsidiaries from the consolidated accounts.

The main reason for wanting to exclude a subsidiary is the desire to engage in off-balance sheet financing (OBF).

One form of OBF involves a "non-subsidiary" borrowing in order to pay for assets which are then made available to the group. That means that neither the assets or liabilities appear in the group accounts and the group's gearing and return on capital employed ratios look better than they otherwise would.

It is generally not acceptable to exclude a subsidiary from the consolidated financial statements. The only exceptions are highly unlikely to occur in practice:

- the holding company might not have effective control

- the subsidiary might be held for resale.

Exam focus

You should understand the definition of a subsidiary in case the exam question asks you to justify the decision to include or exclude a particular company from the group accounts.

5

Consolidated balance sheet

In this chapter

- The basic principle.
- Pre- and post acquisition profits.
- Goodwill on acquisition.
- Minority interest.
- Intra-group trading.
- Unrealised profit on intra-group trading.
- Fair values.
- Mid-year acquisitions.

The basic principle

The basic principle running through the whole topic of consolidation is that we:

- **cancel** all balances that exist between group members **and**

- **combine** the remaining figures **so that**

- **the resulting totals show the assets and liabilities controlled by the group.**

Example

Simplest possible case

P purchased 100% of S's share capital on 31 December 20X4.

Balance sheets at 31 December 20X4

	P	S
	$000	$000
Non-current assets	60	50
Investment in S at cost	50	
Current assets	40	40
	150	90
Ordinary share capital ($1 shares)	100	40
Retained earnings	30	10
Current liabilities	20	40
	150	90

The first thing we have to do is look for relationships within this group.

There is an asset of $50,000 owned by P. This was paid for the net assets in S's balance sheet as at the date this investment was acquired, which is reflected in S's equity of $40,000 in share capital and $10,000 in retained earnings.

Balance sheets at 31 December 20X4

	P	S
	$000	$000
Non-current assets	60	50
Investment in S at cost	50	
Current assets	40	40
	150	90
Ordinary share capital ($1 shares)	100	40
Retained earnings	30	10
Current liabilities	20	40
	150	90

Cancelling these offsetting amounts and combining the remaining figures gives:

P Group

Consolidated balance sheet at 31 December 20X4

	$000
Non-current assets	110
Current assets	80
	190
Ordinary share capital ($1 shares)	100
Retained earnings	30
Current liabilities	60
	190

Exam focus

Even this simple case illustrates the point of consolidated financial statements:

The directors of P control fixed assets of $110,000 in the group as a whole and current assets of $80,000.

Keep a firm grasp of this concept because it may help you to understand the more complicated adjustments that will arise.

Pre- and post- acquisition profits

Key Point

We always cancel the holding company's investment against the subsidiary's equity acquired **as at the date the subsidiary was acquired**.

The subsidiary's retained earnings can be split between those existing 'pre-acquisition' and those that have arisen 'post-acquisition' to help in cancelling these amounts.

Example

Three years later

Balance sheets at 31 December 20X7

	P	S
	$000	$000
Non-current assets	67	58
Investment in S at cost	50	
Current assets	43	45
	160	103
Ordinary share capital ($1 shares)	100	40
Retained earnings	33	14
Current liabilities	27	49
	160	103

We still offset the $50,000 in the holding company books against the $40,000 and $10,000 in the subsidiary's (i.e. we offset the investment against the ordinary shares and pre-acquisition retained earnings):

Workings

retained earnings = 33 + 14-10 = 37

Goodwill on acquisition

There is no reason for the amount paid by the holding company to be equal to the book value of the equity acquired.

Example

Q purchased 100% of T's share capital on 31 December 20X4. On that date T's retained earnings were $50,000.

Balance sheets at 31 December 20X7

	Q	T
	$000	$000
Non-current assets	67	150
Investment in S at cost	145	
Current assets	38	41
	250	191
Ordinary share capital ($1 shares)	150	70
Retained earnings	68	64
Current liabilities	32	57
	250	191

Key Point

Take care with the dates. The balance sheet figures above relate to a period **after** the date of acquisition, so we need to allow for the distinction between pre- and post-acquisition reserves.

Q paid $145,000 for equity in T that was valued at $70,000 + $50,000 = $120,000.

If we cancel $145,000 against $120,000 then the consolidated balance sheet will not balance.

We deal with this by cancelling $120,000 of the investment against the net assets acquired and the remainder is left in the consolidated balance sheet:

Q Group

Consolidated balance sheet at 31 December 20X7

	$000
Intangible fixed assets – goodwill	25
Tangible non-current assets	217
Current assets	79
	321
Ordinary share capital ($1 shares)	150
Retained earnings	82
Current liabilities	89
	321

Workings

Goodwill = $145,000 – 70,000 – 50,000
Retained earnings
= $68,000 + 64,000 – 50,000

The goodwill figure remains in the consolidated balance sheet. IFRS 3 requires that it is not amortised or written off in any way unless the goodwill is affected by an impairment review and has to be written off in whole or in part.

In the unlikely event that goodwill is negative, it should be credited directly to the income statement (i.e. added to retained earnings in the consolidated balance sheet).

Key Point

The figure for goodwill on acquisition does not really mean anything. It remains in the balance sheet indefinitely (unless it is impaired) and becomes increasingly irrelevant for any decision-making purposes.

Minority interest

The holding company might not own all of the subsidiary's share capital.

Any of the subsidiary's equity that is owned by third parties is known as 'minority interest'.

It is treated as an element of equity in the

group financial statements, but it is kept separate from the investment made by the holding company's shareholders.

Example

R purchased 80% of U's share capital on 31 December 20X3. On that date U's retained earnings were $100,000.

	R	U
	$000	$000
Non-current assets	230	270
Investment in U at cost	195	
Current assets	65	80
	490	350
Ordinary share capital ($1 shares)	210	120
Retained earnings	190	160
Current liabilities	90	70
	490	350

It is often a good idea to show the group structure in the form of a diagram (groups can be rather more complicated than a holding company plus a single subsidiary):

R
|
80%
|
U

We have to cancel the $195,000 paid for the subsidiary against the net assets acquired at that date (i.e. 80% of share capital and reserves = $96,000+80,000) = $176,000.

Cancelling this leaves goodwill of $195,000 – 176,000 = $19,000.

The date of acquisition has no significance for the minority shareholders. They are entitled to 20% of all of U's equity as at the balance sheet date = 20% of $120,000+160,000 = $56,000.

The retained earnings in the group balance sheet require some thought. We have cancelled 20% of $100,000 = $20,000 against the investment in the holding company's balance sheet and a further 20%

of $160,000 = $32,000 by classifying it as minority interest.

This means that group retained earnings = $190,000 + 160,000 – 80,000 – 32,000 = $298,000.

R Group

Consolidated balance sheet at 31 December 20X7

	$000
Goodwill	19
Tangible non-current assets	500
Current assets	145
	664
Ordinary share capital ($1 shares)	210
Retained earnings	238
Shareholders' capital	442
Minority interest	56
	504
Current liabilities	160
	664

Exam focus

It is often best to do all of the workings and then to prepare the consolidated statements.

Intra-group trading

If group members trade with one another then the effects of this need to be cancelled.

In the simplest case, one group member will have a trade payable and another will have a trade receivable for the same amount. These balances can simply be offset one against the other.

It can be more complicated when the balances disagree because of delays in recording transactions by one or other party.

Example

R and V are both members of the same group.

At the balance sheet date R showed a trade receivable of $17,000 due from V, while V showed a trade payable of $10,000 due to R.

An investigation showed that R had despatched inventory costing $2,000 just before the year end. This was not received by V until after the year end.

V had sent a cheque for $5,000 just before the year end, but it was not received until just after.

This means that:

- inventory worth $2,000 has been excluded from both balance sheets, even though it belongs to the group
- cash worth $5,000 has been excluded from both balance sheets, because it has been deducted from V's bank account but not added to R's
- the two balances have a discrepancy of $7,000 because of this.

If we assume that the inventory had not been despatched and the cash not paid then we would:

- increase inventory by $2,000
- increase bank by $5,000
- R's receivable would now be $15,000, the same as V's payable – these

balances can now be offset against one another.

Read the adjustments related to inter-company balances carefully. They usually disagree in the question, but there is always sufficient information to reconcile and correct the balances.

Remember that inventory and bank balances will also change in the process.

Unrealised profit on intra-group trading

When group members trade with one another there is usually en element of profit in the transfer price. Indeed, tax rules usually mean that group members have to trade with one another at normal, commercial rates.

This is not a problem if the inventory is subsequently resold to a third party. This means that the group has bought the

inventory at cost and resold it at a mark-up.

The difficulties arise when the inventory remains in one group member's balance sheet at the year end. This means that the group accounts will value the inventory at cost plus an internal mark-up and the group income statement will include the profit from an internal transfer.

Any unrealised profits must be cancelled out before the income statement and balance sheet are prepared.

Example

S sold goods costing $600,000 to its subsidiary W at a transfer price of $720,000. W resold 2/3 of this inventory to third parties before the year end.

The profit element of this transfer is $120,000 ($720,000 − 600,000). One third of this remains in the subsidiary's closing inventory figure. This means that we need to reduce recorded profit and closing inventory by \$120,000 / 3 = \$40,000.

Pay particular attention to the wording of the question in calculating the unrealised profit. Small changes to the wording can affect the way in which this profit is calculated.

If the unrealised profit is in the accounts of a partly owned subsidiary then the adjustment to cancel the unrealised profit will be shared pro-rata between the group and the minority interest.

Fair values

To ensure that an accurate figure is calculated for goodwill:

- the consideration paid for a subsidiary must be accounted for at fair value
- the subsidiary's identifiable assets and liabilities acquired must be accounted for at their fair values.

This can mean that the value of the investment in the subsidiary will have to be calculated in order to determine the investment in the subsidiary.

- Any shares issued should be valued at their market values.
- Any deferred consideration should be discounted back to its net present value.
- Any contingent consideration should be included only if the payment is probable and can be measured reliably.

It also means that any information about the fair values of the net assets acquired must be taken into account when calculating goodwill. Any adjustments will have to be taken into account in determining the non-current assets of the group.

Example

H acquired 80% of the share capital of P two years ago when the reserves of P stood at \$125,000.

H paid an initial cash consideration of $1,000,000. In addition, H issued 200,000 shares with a nominal value of $1.00 and a current market value of $1.80.

It was also agreed that H would pay a further $500,000 in three years' time. Assuming a 10% rate, the appropriate discount factor for $1 receivable in three years from the date of acquisition was 0.751.

The most recent balance sheets of the two companies are shown below:

Balance sheets at 31 December 20X7

	H	P
	$000	$000
Tangabille non-current assets	5,500	1,500
Investment in P	1,736	
Current assets	1,150	350
	3,386	1,850

Share capital	2,200	500
Share premium	160	–
Retained earnings	1,400	300
	3,760	800
Non-current liabilities	3,376	400
Current liabilities	1,250	650
	3,386	1,850

At the date of acquisition the fair value of P's non-current assets exceeded their book value by $200,000. These assets had a remaining useful life of five years at that date. This revaluation was not reflected in P's books.

One fifth of the goodwill on acquisition has been written off because of impairment.

The investment in P is made up:

Cash	1,000,000
Shares (= 200,000 × $1.80)	360,000
Deferred consideration (= $500,000 × 0.751)	375,500
	1,735,500

(Rounded to $1,736,000.)

The workings to support the consolidated balance sheet are as follows:

H
|
90%
|
P

Goodwill

Fair value of consideration = $1,736,000

Acquired:

Share capital (90% of $500,000)	$450,000
Retained earnings (90% of $125,000)	112,500
Fair value adjustments (90% of $200,000)	180,000
	$742,500

Goodwill (1,736–742 rounded)	$994,000
Impairment of goodwill ($993,000/5)	$198,600
Remaining goodwill	$795,400

Additional depreciation of non-current assets:

(2/5 of $200,000)	$80,000
Split – 90% group	$72,000
– 10% minority interest	$8,000

Tangible fixed assets	
H	$5,500,000
P	1,500,000
Fair value adjustment	200,000
Depreciation	(80,000)
	7,120,000

Retained earnings	
H	$1,400,000
P	300,000
Less: cancelled against investment	(112,500)
Less: impairment of goodwill	(198,600)
Less: additional depreciation	(72,000)
Less: minority interest	(30,000)
	1,286,900

Minority interest	
Share capital (10%)	$50,000
Retained earnings (10%)	30,000
Revaluation	
(10% of $200,000 less 2/5)	12,000
	$92,000

H Group

Consolidated balance sheet at 31 December 20X7

	$000
Goodwill on acquisition	795
Tangible non-current assets	7,120
Current assets	1,500
	9,415
Share capital	2,200
Share premium	160
Retained earnings	1,287
Shareholders' investment	3,647
Minority interest	92
Non-current liabilities	3,776
Current liabilities	1,900
	9,415

Mid-year acquisitions

If an acquisition takes place during the year then the net assets as at the date of acquisition must be estimated.

This might involve assuming that the profit or loss of the subsidiary accrued evenly throughout the year so as to determine retained profits part-way between the beginning of the year and the year-end.

Exam focus

The key to consolidation questions is the preparation of clear and straightforward workings.

If you understand what you are trying to do then you will have very little difficulty in preparing workings to suit.

6

Consolidated income statement

In this chapter

- The basic principles.
- Dividends.
- Mid-year acquisitions.

The basic principles

There are three basic principles:

- Adjust for any intra-group items such as inter-company sales or dividends.
- The figures down to profit after tax equal the total of the group members' figures, adjusted for any intra-group items.
- The minority interest in the profit for the year is deducted from profit after tax.

Exam focus

The important thing is to read the question very carefully in order to decide which adjustments affect the balance brought forward on the retained earnings as opposed to those that affect the profit for the year.

Dividends

Any dividend income received by the holding company from a subsidiary will have to be cancelled.

This can complicate the statement of changes in equity, bearing in mind that the minority interest in the consolidated income statement is based on profit after tax – some of that figure will be paid as a dividend and the remainder will be credited to the minority interest balance.

Example

Use the following information to prepare a consolidated income statement and a reconciliation of retained earnings for the P group for the year ended 31 December 20X7.

P paid $1.5 million for 80% of L's share capital of $800,000. The balance on L's retained earnings was $600,000 at that time.

Goodwill impairments charged during the periods since the acquisition but prior to this year amounted to $152,000. A further impairment of $38,000 was found to be necessary at the year end. Impairments are included within administrative expenses.

P made sales of $600,000 to L during the year. Not all of the goods had been sold to third parties by the year end. The profit element included in L's closing inventory was $30,000.

The figure for investment income in P's income statement comprises the parent company's share of the subsidiary's total dividend for the year.

Income statements for the year ended 31 December 20X7

	P	L
	$000	$000
Sales revenue	3,200	2,560
Cost of sales	2,200	1,480
Gross profit	1,000	1,080
Distribution costs	160	120
Administrative expenses	400	80
	440	880
Investment income	160	–
	600	880
Taxation	400	480
	200	400
Additional infromation		
Dividend paid	96	200
Retained profit b/fwd	1,200	1,120

The basic approach is very similar to that of preparing a consolidated balance sheet.

We might have had to calculate goodwill on acquisition, but the figures for the amounts written off have been given in the question.

If there had been any fair value adjustments on the acquisition then these would have had to be taken into account in calculating any additional depreciation in dealing with the retained earnings brought forward and any additional charges for the year.

Workings

Sales revenue
(3,200 + 2,560 – 600) $5,160,000

Cost of sales
(2,200 + 1,480 – 600 + 30) $3,110,000

Administrative expenses
(400 + 80 + 38) $518,000

Minority interest for year
(20% of 400) $80,000

Retained profit brought forward:

- P $1,200,000
- L   1,120,000
- Cancelled on acquisition
  (80% of 600)   (480,000)
- Minority interest (20% of 1,120)   (224,000)
- Goodwill amortisation   (152,000)

                                         $1,464,000

P Group

Consolidated income statement for the year ended 31 December 20X7

	$000
Sales revenue	5,160
Cost of sales	3,110
Gross profit	2,050
Distribution costs	280
Administrative expenses	518
	1,252
Tax	880
Net profit after tax	372
Minority interest	80
Profit for the year	292

Movement on consolidated retained earnings

	$000
Consolidated retained earnings brought forward	1,464
Profit for the period	292
Dividends paid	(96)
	1,660

Mid-year acquisitions

As with the balance sheet, if the subsidiary is acquired during the year then the figures in the income statement should reflect the results for the part of the year for which the subsidiary was part of the group.

If necessary, the figures could be calculated pro-rata.

Exam focus

The process for preparing the consolidated income statement is exactly the same as that for the consolidated balance sheet.

Appreciating the logic behind the adjustments will make it much easier to remember and apply them.

7

Associates

In this chapter

- IAS 28 Investments in associates.
- Equity accounting.
- Consolidated balance sheet.
- Sundry points.

IAS 28 investments in associates

Definition

IAS 28 defines an **associate** as:

An entity over which the investor has significant influence and that is neither a subsidiary nor an interest in joint venture.

Significant influence is the power to participate in the financial and operating policy decisions of the investee but is not control or joint control over those policies.

Exam focus

The definition of significant influence is very broad. You might have to read the question very carefully in order to decide whether an investment creates an associate.

It is normally assumed that significant influence exists if the holding company has a shareholding of 20% to 50%. That does not,

however, guarantee that the holding company has any real influence. For example, a 40% shareholding might actually offer very little real influence if the remaining 60% is in the hands of another individual shareholder.

Equity accounting

Key Point

Acquisition accounting is used to account for subsidiaries.

Equity accounting is used to account for associates.

Unlike acquisition accounting, which combined the holding company's figures with those of the subsidiary or subsidiaries, equity accounting involves single figure adjustments to the consolidated income statement and the consolidated balance sheet.

Key Point

The consolidated income statement includes the **investor's share** of the associate's results.

The consolidated balance sheet includes the **investor's share** of the associate's net assets.

The holding company is not required to produce consolidated statements unless it has at least one subsidiary. Associates are accounted for using equity accounting within the consolidated financial statements, but the existence of an associate does not, in itself, require the preparation of group accounts.

Consolidated balance sheet

The initial investment in the associate is shown at cost, identifying any goodwill on acquisition.

The carrying amount is then adjusted to include the group share of any profits arising post-acquisition, less any goodwill written off through impairment.

Alternatively, the same figure can be determined by taking the group's share of the associate's net assets at the balance sheet date and adding any goodwill that is not yet impaired.

Example

Hold acquired 80% of Sub when Sub's retained losses were $56,000.

Hold acquired 30% of Ass when Ass' retained earnings were $140,000.

An impairment test has determined that goodwill on the acquisition of Sub has been impaired by $3,360,000 and that of Ass by $2,800,000.

The latest balance sheets of the group members are as follows:

Balance sheets as at 31 December 20X9

	Hold Ltd $000	Sub Ltd $000	Ass Ltd $000
Tangible non-current assets	1,120	980	840
Investment in Sub	644		
Investment in Ass	224		
Current assets	605	1,008	336
	2,593	1,988	1,176
Share capital	1,120	840	560
Retained earnings	1,232	602	448
	2,352	1,442	1,008
Current liabilities	241	546	168
	2,593	1,988	1,176

The group structure is:

Hold

80%   30%

Sub   Ass

Sub is undoubtedly under Hold's control and is, therefore, a subsidiary.

Ass is undoubtedly subject to significant influence, which makes the company an associate.

Goodwill on the acquisition of Sub	
Investment	$644,000
Share capital (80% of 840)	672,000
Reserves (80% of -56)	(44,800)
Goodwill	$16,800
Less: amortisation	$3,360
	$13,440

Goodwill on the acquisition of Ass	
Investment	$224,000
Share capital (30% of 560)	168,000
Reserves (30% of 140)	42,000
Goodwill	$14,000

Minority interest in Sub	
Share capital (20% of 840)	$168,000
Retained earnings (20% of 602)	120,400
Minority interest	$288,400

Investment in associate	
Cost	$224,000
Group share of post-acquisition profit (30% of 448-140)	92,400
Impairment of goodwill	(2,800)
	$313,600

Retained earnings	
Hold	$1,232,000
Sub	602,000
Cancelled against investment	44,800
Goodwill amortised (3,360 + 2,800)	(6,160)
Minority interest	(120,400)
	1,752,240
Group share of associate's post-acquisition	92,400
	$1,844,640

Hold Group

Consolidated balance sheet as at
31 December 20X9

	$
Goodwill	13,440
Tangible non-current assets	2,100,000
Investment in Ass	313,600
Current assets	1,613,000
	4,040,040
Share capital	1,120,000
Retained earnings	1,844,640
Shareholders' equity	2,964,640
Minority interest	288,400
	3,253,040
Current liabilities	787,000
	4,040,040

Key Point

Only the holding company and subsidiaries are included in the consolidated asset and liability figures.

The associate is a single line item only.

Sundry points

The accounting treatment of associates has some similarities to accounting for subsidiaries, but there are also some significant differences.

Key Point

Associates are not members of the group in the same way that subsidiaries are.

Always remember that subsidiaries are **controlled** by the holding company, whereas associates are subject to no more than **significant interest**.

Fair values

If the fair value of the associate's net assets at acquisition are materially different from their book value the net assets should be adjusted in the same way as for a subsidiary.

Balances with the associate

Generally the associate is considered to be outside the group. Therefore balances between group companies and the associate will remain in the consolidated balance sheet.

If a group company trades with the associate, the resulting payables and receivables will remain in the consolidated balance sheet.

Sales to and from associates

Sales between group members and associates are left in the consolidated income statement. The only adjustments are in respect of any closing inventory that remains from such transactions.

Unrealised profit in inventory

Unrealised profit in closing inventory arising from sales between group members and associates should still be cancelled.

If the sale was made to the associate then the amount of the unrealised profit should be added back to group cost of sales.

If the sale was made by the associate then it would be more appropriate to deduct the unrealised profit from the group's share of the associate's profit. However, it would be acceptable to make the adjustment to the group cost of sales for the sake of simplicity.

Dividends from associates

Dividends from associates are not included in the consolidated income statement. This is because the dividend is effectively being paid out of the group's share of the associate's profit, which has already been recognised in the group accounts.

Presentation of financial statements

In this chapter

- IAS 1 Presentation of financial statements.
- IFRS 5 Non-current assets held for sale and discontinued operations.
- Discontinued operations.

IAS 1 Presentation of financial statements

Exam focus

Question 2 will always cover the preparation of financial statements. The question may not require the preparation of a full set of accounts, but it will always be worthwhile to be prepared to do so if the need arises.

Income statement

The following format is taken from the appendix to IAS 1. It shows a model income statement for a group, but a single-entity's statement would be identical, but for the removal of references to associates, parents and minority interests.

	$
Revenue	X
Cost of sales	(X)
Gross profit	X
Other income	X
Distribution costs	(X)
Administrative expenses	(X)
Other expenses	(X)
Finance costs	(X)
Share of profit of associate	X
Profit before tax	X
Tax expense	(X)
Profit for the period	X
Attributable to:	
Equity holders of the parent	X
Minority interests	X
	X

Balance sheet

As before, this format is suitable for a group, but could easily be converted to that of a single-entity by removing the references to group members.

ASSETS	$
Non-Current Assets	
Property, plant and equipment	X
Goodwill	X
Other intangible assets	X
Investment in associates	X
Available for sale investments	X
	X
Current Assets	
Inventories	X
Trade receivables	X
Other current assets	X
Cash and cash equivalents	X
	X
Total assets	X

EQUITY AND LIABILITIES

Equity Attributable to Equity Holders of Parent	
Share capital	X
Other reserves	X
Retained earnings	X
	X
Minority interest	X
Total equity	X
Non-current liabilities	
Long-term borrowings	X
Deferred tax	X
Long-term provisions	X
	X
Current liabilities	
Trade and other payables	X
Short-term borrowings	X
Current portion of long-term borrowings	X
Current tax payable	X
Short-term provisions	X
	X
Total liabilities	X
Total equity and liabilities	X

Key Point

The secret to questions involving the preparation of financial statements is practice, followed by more practice.

If you attempt as many of these questions as you possibly can while studying and revising for the exam then you will find that the preparation becomes second nature.

Exam focus

Don't worry if you make the odd slip of presentation or layout. There are relatively few marks for the formats and their application.

The main reason for knowing the IAS 1 formats well is that they will enable you to attempt questions quickly and efficiently.

Statement of changes in equity

This shows the movements on reserves for the period under consideration.

Again, practice makes perfect.

	Attributes to Equity Holders of the parent					Minority interests	Total Equity
	Share Capital	Share premium	Other Reserves	Retained Earnings	Total		
	$	$	$	$	$	$	$
Opening balance	X	X	X	X	X	X	X
Changes in accounting policy	–	–	–	(X)	(X)	–	(X)
Restated balance	X	X	X	X	X	X	X
Changes in equity for year							
Minority in new subsidiary	–	–	–	–	–	X	X
Property revaluation gains	–	–	X	–	X	–	X
Investment valuation gains (losses)	–	–	–	(X)	(X)	–	(X)
Tax on items taken to equity	–	–	(X)	X	(X)	–	(X)
Net income recognised directly in equity	–	–	X	X	X	X	X
Profit for the period	–	–	–	X	X	X	X
Total recognised income and expense for the period	–	–	X	X	X	X	X
Dividends	–	–	–	(X)	(X)	(X)	(X)
Issue of share capital	X	X	–	–	–	–	X
Closing balance	X	X	X	X	X	X	X

IFRS 5 Non-current assets held for sale and discontinued operations

A non-current asset should be classified as 'held for sale' if its carrying amount will be recovered principally through a sale transaction rather than through continuing use.

For this to be the case, the following conditions must apply:

- the asset must be available for immediate sale in its present condition
- the sale must be highly probable, meaning that:
- management are committed to a plan to sell the asset
- there is an active programme to locate a buyer; and
- the asset is being actively marketed
- the sale is expected to be completed within 12 months of its classification as held for sale
- it is unlikely that the plan will be significantly changed or will be withdrawn.

Key Point

Non-current assets that qualify as held for sale should be measured at the lower of their carrying amount and fair value less costs to sell.

Held for sale non-current assets should be presented separately on the face of the balance sheet and not depreciated.

Discontinued operations

A discontinued operation is a component of an enterprise that either has been disposed of, or is classified as held for sale, and:

- represents a separate major line of business or geographical area of operations

- is part of a single co-ordinated plan to dispose of a separate major line of business or geographical area of operations, or

- is a subsidiary acquired exclusively with a view to resale.

Discontinued operations are required to be shown separately in order to help users to predict future performance, i.e. based upon continuing operations.

Tangible non-current assets

In this chapter

- IAS 16 Property, plant and equipment.
- IAS 23 Borrowing costs.
- IAS 20 Accounting for government grants and disclosure of government assistance.
- IAS 40 Investment properties.

IAS 16

Questions at this level are as likely to ask you to explain and justify the rules in the relevant IAS as to ask you to apply those rules.

IAS 16 Property, plant and equipment deals with most of the issues associated with non-current assets.

Is it an asset?

One of the biggest problems that arises in the real world is the decision as to whether an item of expenditure was to acquire a non-current asset ("capital expenditure") or whether it should be treated as an expense ("revenue expenditure").

Questions might test your ability to distinguish capital expenditure from revenue.

IAS 16 provides some pointers, although these often don't give a clear and definitive treatment.

There is often scope for disagreement.

Don't worry if you are not 100% sure how something should be treated in the application of IAS 16. marks are as likely to be awarded for the reasoning behind your treatment as the treatment itself.

Firstly, does the expenditure meet the recognition criteria for an item of property, plant and equipment?

- Is it probable that future economic benefits associated with the asset will flow to the enterprise?

- Can the cost of the asset can be measured reliably?

If the outlay meets both of these criteria then it is probably appropriate to treat the outlay as capital expenditure.

If this is a completely new asset then the capitalised cost should include all of the costs involved in bringing the asset to its working condition (e.g. you should include delivery and installation costs) but you should exclude any element that should be treated as revenue expenditure (e.g. a tank full of petrol in a new van).

Any subsequent expenditure on existing property, plant and equipment should meet the same recognition criteria.

- Repairs and running costs should always be written off as revenue expenditure.
- Improvements (e.g. an extension to a building) will almost always be capitalised.
- Large outlays incurred during the course of an asset's life (e.g. a major refit of a ship) have to be analysed on a case-by-case basis and may or may not be capital expenditure.

Depreciation

Definition

Depreciation is the systematic allocation of the depreciable amount of an asset over its useful life.

Depreciable amount is the cost of an asset, or other amount substituted for cost in the financial statements, less its residual value.

Exam focus

Read the question carefully, the examiner will tell you how depreciation is to be calculated.

All non-current assets with finite useful lives must be depreciated.

Assets should be depreciated over their remaining lives, whether they are shown at cost less depreciation to date or at a valuation.

If the question requires a change to the depreciation approach, whether that be an alteration to the estimated life or even a switch from one method to another (e.g. straight line to reducing balance) then that should be treated as a change in an accounting estimate rather than a change of accounting policy.

Revaluations

The mechanics of revaluation are very straightforward.

- Restate the cost/valuation to the revalued amount.

- Restate the accumulated depreciation on the asset to zero.

- The net increase/decrease is the gain/loss on revaluation.

A **gain on revaluation** is credited to the revaluation reserve (via the statement of changes in equity).

A **loss on revaluation** is usually[1] charged to the income statement as an expense.

Depreciation is subsequently based on the revalued amount.

If a company decides to show one asset at valuation then it is required to revalue all of the assets in that category (e.g. all land and buildings). This is to prevent companies from 'cherry-picking' assets that have increased in value to be shown at valuation while leaving those that would have decreased at their cost less depreciation.

Once a category of assets has been revalued then the valuations have to be kept reasonably up to date.

---

[1] If the asset had previously been revalued at a gain then part of any subsequent loss on revaluation can be deducted from the revaluation reserve, up to the amount that had previously been credited in respect of the asset.

Disclosures

For each class of depreciable asset disclosure must be made of:

- depreciation methods used
- useful lives or depreciation rates used
- total depreciation charged for the period
- gross amount of depreciable assets and related accumulated
- depreciation
- if material, the reason for any change in depreciation method.

For revalued assets:

- name and qualification of valuer
- basis of the valuation
- date and amount of valuations.

IAS 23

IAS 23 Borrowing costs deals with the question of whether finance costs incurred in the construction of a building can be capitalised.

IAS 23's preferred treatment is to write off all finance charges as they are incurred. It is, however, permissible to capitalise certain costs.

Exam focus

The examiner might expect you to offer opinions or justifications for the accounting treatment required by particular IASs or IFRSs.

It might make sense to capitalise interest associated with the construction of a building (or any other asset that takes a long time to get ready). Arguably, the borrowing costs could be seen as part of the cost in exactly the same way as the cost of the materials or labour applied.

On the other hand, it might be difficult to identify the actual costs of borrowing associated with this asset (unless the company took out a loan that was specifically for this purpose). It can also lead to inconsistencies (such as two identical buildings having different carrying values because one was financed with debt and the other with equity).

Key Point

If you do have to justify the treatment adopted by a standard then think about its impact on the financial statements.

- Will it increase reported profit?
- What will it do to the balance sheet?
- Do you believe that these are improvements?

It is permissible to capitalise borrowing costs incurred during the period when work is in progress on the asset. Costs incurred after the asset has been completed or while work is suspended must be written off as revenue expenditure.

It is also necessary that expenditure on the asset and associated borrowing costs are being incurred.

Capitalised borrowing costs are those actually incurred, although this might have to be estimated if the entity is financing the cost out of general borrowings.

The disclosures required by IAS 23 are:

- the accounting policy adopted for borrowing costs
- the amount of borrowing costs capitalised during the period
- the capitalisation rate used.

IAS 20

IAS 20 Accounting for government grants and disclosure of government assistance deals with grants, which may or may not be provided in support of the acquisition of a non-current asset.

Grants can either be in respect of capital or revenue expenditure.

IAS 20 permits a grant to be treated in one of two ways.

Revenue grants

(e.g. a government contribution towards the cost of wages) can **either**:

- be presented as a credit in the income statement **or**

- be deducted from the related expense.

Capital grants

(e.g. a government contribution towards the cost of a new piece of machinery) can **either**:

- be written off against the cost of the associated non-current asset, with depreciation then based on the resulting reduced cost **or**

- be treated as a deferred credit in the liabilities section of the balance sheet and a portion transferred to revenue each year, so offsetting the depreciation that will have been calculated based on the original cost.

Exam focus

You are free to choose whichever treatment you deem more appropriate (or simpler), unless the examiner specifies a particular treatment for a grant.

IAS 40

IAS 40 Investment properties excludes certain properties from the requirement that all non-current assets with finite lives be depreciated.

Definition

Investment property is land or a building held to earn rentals, or for capital appreciation or both, rather than for use in the enterprise or for sale in the ordinary course of business.

Owner-occupied property is excluded from the definition of investment property.

Investment properties should initially be measured at cost.

IAS 40 then gives a choice between following:

- a cost model
- a fair value model.

Once the model is chosen it should be used for all investment properties.

Under the cost model, investment properties are shown at cost less depreciation as for any other non-current asset.

Under the fair value model the asset is revalued to fair value at the end of each year. The gain or loss on revaluation is shown directly in the income statement and no depreciation is charged on the asset.

Fair value is normally established by reference to current prices on an active market for properties of in the same location and condition.

10

Intangible assets

In this chapter

- IAS 38 Intangible assets.
- Goodwill.
- Research and development.

IAS 38

IAS 38 Intangible assets deals with similar issues to those raised by IAS 16.

Key Point

The main difference between tangible and intangible assets from an accounting point of view is that the recognition criteria for intangibles are more complex and the determination of useful lives can be equally problematic.

Definition

An intangible asset is an identifiable non-monetary asset without physical substance.

In order to be "identifiable" the asset has to be separable from the rest of the business or arising from legal rights. Thus, a patent could be an intangible asset on both grounds, but the company's "good name and reputation" could not (even though it might be far more valuable).

Recognition

IAS 38 uses the same recognition criteria as those used in IAS 16 for tangible non-current assets.

- Is it probable that future economic benefits associated with the asset will flow to the enterprise?
- Can the cost of the asset can be measured reliably?

These criteria effectively restrict the recognition of intangible assets to those that have been purchased. It is generally regarded as impossible to separate the costs of internally-generated intangibles from the business' normal running costs and so there is no reliable measure.

Measurement after recognition

IAS 38 permits intangibles to be shown at either cost less amortisation or at valuation.

Cost less amortisation is more common.

The valuation approach is only permissible where a fair value can be determined by reference to an active market. This means that the asset has to be homogenous and freely traded in an observable marketplace.

Key Point

You might be able to see parallels between the treatment adopted in each of the IASs and IFRSs mentioned in this text and the Framework discussed in chapter 2.

The Framework is often a good place to start when the examiner asks you to discuss a particular standard.

Amortisation

An intangible asset with a finite useful life must be amortised over that life, normally using the straight-line method with a zero residual value.

An intangible asset with an indefinite useful life should not be amortised, but should be tested for impairment annually. (Impairment will be discussed in chapter 11.)

Disclosures

The following disclosures should be made with respect to each class of intangibles:

- whether the useful lives are finite or indefinite
- the useful lives or the amortisation rates used for assets with finite lives
- the amortisation methods used for assets with finite lives.

Goodwill

Definition

Goodwill is the difference between the value of a business as a whole and the aggregate of the fair values of its separable net assets.

Goodwill can be the most valuable asset owned by a company, but it is only recognised when it is purchased.

Purchased goodwill arises most frequently in the context of the acquisition of a subsidiary and is dealt with in IFRS 3.

Goodwill purchased under any other circumstances would be dealt with under the provisions of IAS 38.

Research and development

R&D is dealt with under the provisions of IAS 38.

Key Point

This is a complicated area in practice and requires particular consideration.

Definition

Research is original and planned investigation undertaken with the prospect of gaining new scientific knowledge and understanding.

Definition

Development is the application of research findings or other knowledge to a plan or design for the production of new or substantially improved materials, devices, products, processes, systems or services before the start of commercial production or use.

The distinction between research and development can be crucial for accounting purposes because development costs can be capitalised whereas research costs cannot.

IAS 38 lays down stringent criteria for the treatment of expenditure as development. These can be summed up as requiring clear evidence that the project is both technically and commercially viable. If there is any doubt that the development work will not lead to a viable product then the costs should be written off.

Only costs incurred after a project has

been recognised as development can be recognised as such. This means that any costs incurred at the earlier stages, when the work would have been classified as research, remain written off as expenses.

IAS 38's rules on the amortisation and disclosure of intangibles apply to development.

11

Impairment of assets

In this chapter

- IAS 36 Impairment of assets.

IAS 36

IAS 36 Impairment of assets is intended to avoid the possibility that non-current assets (whether tangible or intangible) are carried at excessive amounts in the balance sheet.

An asset is impaired if it is worth less than its book value.

'Worth' is determined in terms of its **recoverable amount**.

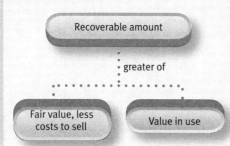

Recoverable amount

greater of

Fair value, less costs to sell

Value in use

The recoverable amount is essentially based on the logical way to treat the asset.

The recoverable amount is based on a comparison of the net amount that could be obtained from selling an asset and the net present value of the cash flows that it will generate.

For example, a piece of machinery could be sold for $1,000 after allowing for selling expenses. The machine's cash flows have a net present value of $1,200.

It makes sense to keep this asset rather than sell it, so the asset's recoverable amount is $1,200.

IAS 36 requires that an impairment review be conducted whenever a balance sheet is prepared. In practice, this does not necessarily involve an enormous amount of work. Generally companies use common sense to decide whether or not a detailed impairment review is required.

- If assets are generally valued at cost less depreciation or at fair values determined in a reasonably conservative way then there is very little likelihood that they will have been impaired.

- Impairment is far more likely to occur when there has been a major upheaval in a market or industry.

Key Point

Impairment losses are charged to the income statement, except to the extent that they reverse a previously-recognised gain on revaluation, in which case that part will go to the revaluation reserve.

Cash generating units

It is not always possible to base the impairment review on individual assets.

For example, it might be impossible to estimate the net present value of the cash flows that might be generated by each separate piece of machinery in a factory production line. It might make more sense to evaluate the whole production line as a single cash generating unit (CGU) and conduct the impairment review for the CGU as a whole.

This is particularly relevant in dealing with purchased goodwill. The annual impairment review for purchased goodwill would have to be conducted for the CGU (which would probably be the subsidiary or the business that had been purchased in order to acquire the goodwill).

If a CGU is impaired then the goodwill allocated to the CGU should be written down first and the remainder of the write-down applied to other assets in proportion to their carrying value.

12

Inventories and construction contracts

In this chapter

- IAS 2 Inventory valuation.
- IAS 11 Construction contracts.

IAS 2

Key Point

IAS 2 Inventory valuation requires that inventories should be valued at the lower of cost and net realisable value.

Exam focus

At this level, the examiner might be more interested in your ability to determine cost in a complex case than to be able to describe the rules.

Cost includes all of the costs associated with bringing items of inventory to their present condition and location.

Cost includes:

- purchase price including import duties, transport and handling costs

- any other directly attributable costs, less trade discounts, rebates and subsidies

- costs which are specifically attributable to units of production, e.g. direct labour, direct expenses and subcontracted work

- production overheads (which must be based on the normal level of activity)

- other overheads, if any, attributable in the particular circumstances of the business to bringing the product or service to its present location and condition.

Cost excludes:

- abnormal waste

- storage costs

- administrative overheads which do not contribute to bringing inventories to their present location and condition

- selling costs.

Some businesses can identify individual units of inventory (e.g. vehicles can be identified by a chassis number). Those that cannot should keep track of costs using either the first in, first out (FIFO) or the weighted average cost

Chapter 12

(AVCO) assumption.

The main disclosure requirements of IAS 2 are:

- accounting policy adopted, including the cost formula used
- total carrying amount, classified appropriately
- amount of inventories carried at NRV
- amount of inventories recognised as an expense during the period
- details of any circumstances that have led to the write-down of inventories to their NRV.

IAS 11

IAS 11 Construction contracts deals with the recognition of revenues and balances associated with long-term projects carried out for clients.

Key Point

The logic behind IAS 11 is that long term contracts are deemed to be "sold" to clients throughout the course of each contract.

If, say, 75% of a potentially profitable contract has been completed to date then 75% of the profit anticipated on that contract should have been recognised during the income statement(s) covering the period(s) since work on the contract commenced.

Cumulative revenues and costs that have already been recognised are deducted from the total as at the year end to give the revenue and cost for the year.

Any expected losses on contracts should be recognised as expenses immediately.

Contract revenue comprises:

- the initial revenue agreed with the client
- any additional variations or claims that are probably going to result in revenue

and that can be measured reliably

Contract costs comprise:

- costs that relate directly to the specific contract
- costs that are attributable to contract activity in general and can be allocated to the contract
- such other costs as are specifically chargeable to the customer under the terms of the contract.

Exam focus

The examiner will tell you the basis upon which to determine the stage of completion of each contract and the basis upon which profit to date is to be recognised.

The balance sheet will include the gross amount due from/to customers as an asset/ liability. This can be determined as:

	$
Costs incurred	X
Add: recognised profit	X
Less: recognised losses	(X)
Less: progress billings	(X)
Gross amount due to/from customers	X

Any unpaid progress billings will be treated as trade receivables.

13

Financial assets and financial liabilities/ contracts

In this chapter

- IAS 39 Financial Instruments: Recognition and Measurement.
- IAS 32 Financial Instruments: Presentation.

Financial instruments

This has been a controversial area in practice. At one time there was a huge industry associated with the creation of complex financial instruments that had a distorting effect on the balance sheets of the companies that used them.

Key Point

The main problem has been that debt generally makes balance sheets look weaker. In the past a great deal of ingenuity was put into the creation of financial statements that made debt less visible.

This improved gearing ratios, but in an artificial way because the company was liable for a higher debt than the balance sheet acknowledged.

IAS 39

IAS 39 Financial Instruments: Recognition and Measurement requires that an enterprise should recognise a financial asset or a financial liability on its balance sheet:

- when, and only when, it becomes a party to the contractual provisions of the instrument
- at cost, i.e. the fair value of the consideration given or received for it plus transaction costs.

Financial instruments should be derecognised as follows:

- financial asset – when, and only when, the contractual rights provided by the asset expire or the enterprise loses control of the contractual rights that comprise the financial asset
- financial liability – when, and only when, the obligation specified in the contract is discharged, cancelled or expires.

On derecognition:

- the difference between the carrying amount of the asset or liability, and the amount received or paid for it, should be included in the profit or loss for the period.

Measurement of financial liabilities

Exam focus

The requirements of IAS 39 are largely beyond the scope of the Paper F7 Syllabus but you may be required to value debt issues.

Key Point

The logic behind IAS 39's treatment is to value liabilities and their associated finance charges in relation to the actual cash flows rather than any nominal interest rates agreed in the contract with the lender.

The effective interest rate associated with a financial instrument is basically the internal

rate of return of the cash flows associated with the instrument.

For example

- A company sold bonds with a face value of $1m at a 60% discount.
- Issue costs amounted to $50,000.
- No interest is payable, but the bonds will be redeemed at par in ten years time.
- This is accounted for on the basis that the company received a net cash sum of $350,000 ($1m, less 60%, less issue costs of $50,000). That will be recognised as the initial liability.
- The IRR of these cash flows (an inflow of $350,000 at year 0 and an outflow of $1m in year 10) is 11.069%.
- We will account for this instrument as a loan of $350,000 with an interest charge of 11.069% throughout the life of the instrument.

If the examiner does not give you the IRR then the cash flows will have to be very simple so that you can determine it easily from annuity or net present value tables in the exam.

IAS 32

IAS 32 Financial Instruments: Presentation classifies financial instruments as debt or equity according to the substance of the contractual arrangement.

Key Point

It does not matter whether a financial instrument is called a 'share' or 'equity'. IAS 32 might still classify it as a liability if it has the characteristics of debt.

A financial instrument is classified as **debt** if the issuer has a contractual obligation either to deliver cash or another financial asset to the holder or to exchange another financial asset/liability with the holder under conditions that are potentially unfavourable to the issuer.

A financial instrument is classified as **equity** if it does not give rise to such a contractual obligation.

For example, preference shares:

- are classified as equity if they are irredeemable
- are classified as debt if they are redeemable.

Compound instruments

A compound instrument is one which has both a liability and an equity component.

For example, a convertible bond pays interest for the first part of its life, at which time it is redeemed or converted into ordinary share capital. The interest paid during the debt phase is usually lower than the rate offered on equivalent debt capital that does not carry conversion rights.

Compound instruments must be broken down between their liability element and equity element and each is shown in the appropriate part of the balance sheet. This is usually accomplished by subtracting the net present value of the cash payments associated with the debt element from the fair value of the proceeds of issuing the instrument. That remainder is the equity element.

14

Leases

In this chapter

- IAS 17 Leases.

IAS 17

IAS 17 Leases deals with a complicated area that was frequently used to disguise liabilities in the balance sheet.

The point of IAS 17 is to identify those leases that are effectively financial instruments used to acquire the rights and benefits associated with a particular asset. These are then classified as liabilities in the balance sheet.

Not all leases have to be treated in this way. Some leases do not give the lessee the rights and benefits of ownership (e.g. when a business hires a van for a week).

Definition

A **finance lease** is a lease that transfers substantially all the risks and rewards incidental to ownership of an asset to the lessee.

Definition

An **operating lease** is any lease other than a finance lease.

Exam focus

Leasing questions often ask you to explain why a particular agreement should be treated as a finance lease or an operating lease. The question will imply one or the other in terms of whether the lessee has the risks and rewards of ownership.

In general, a lease is a finance lease if:

- the leased asset is likely to become the property of the lessee at the end of the agreement (either automatically or because there is an option that is likely to be exercised)

- the lease (including any secondary term that is likely to be taken up) is likely to run for most of the asset's useful life

- the present value of the minimum lease

payments is close to the fair value of the asset at the commencement of the lease

- the asset is of a specialised nature that makes it particularly suited to the lessee.

This list is not intended to be exhaustive. Every question has to be approached on its own terms.

Substance over form

The treatment required by IAS 17 effectively accounts for the economic substance of finance leases rather than their legal form.

The economic substance is that the lessee has borrowed an amount equivalent to the fair value of the asset and used that sum to purchase the asset itself. The fact that the lessee may never become the legal owner of the asset is ignored.

Accounting for finance leases

At the start of the lease:

- the fair value (or, if lower, the present value of the minimum lease payments) should be included as a non-current asset, subject to depreciation

- the same amount (being the obligation to pay rentals) should be included as a loan, i.e. a liability.

In practice, the fair value of the asset or its cash price will often be a sufficiently close approximation to the present value of the minimum lease payments and therefore can be used instead.

The asset is depreciated over the shorter of the asset's useful life and the term of the lease (including any secondary term that is likely to be taken up).

Each lease payment is split between:

- a repayment of the lease liability
- a finance charge.

The examiner will have to tell you how to split lease payments between capital repayments and finance charges.

Questions normally state the interest rate implicit in the lease. This makes it easy to determine the finance charges that were incurred during the period. This approach is called the "actuarial method".

If the interest rate implicit in the lease is not stated then it might be possible to derive it if the cash flows are sufficiently simple. It is just the internal rate of return of the cash flows. Alternatively, it is possible to make a crude estimate by using the "sum of the digits" method.

Example

Actuarial method

An asset with a fair value of $5,710 is leased for four years, with the option to continue the lease for a further four years at a negligible 'peppercorn' rent. The asset's useful life is nine years.

Lease payments of $2,000 are made annually at the end of every year for the first four years.

The interest rate implicit in this lease is 15%.

Read the details about the cash flows very carefully. In particular, make sure that you know whether the lease payments should be deducted at the beginning of the period or the end.

If the lease is to be treated as a finance lease then the asset will be capitalised at $5,710 at the start of year 1. It will be depreciated over eight years (the secondary term is likely to be taken up).

The first year's interest will be based on 15% of $5,710 = $856.

The first lease payment of \$2,000 can be split \$856 finance charge and \$1,144 capital.

At the end of the first year, we will have a liability of \$5,710 − 1,144 = \$4,566.

We need to split the liability between current and non-current liabilities. We do this by determining the capital that is to be repaid in year two:

- Year two's finance charge = 15% of \$4,566 = \$685.
- Year two's capital repayment = \$2,000 − 685 = \$1,315.

At the end of year one, the total liability on the lease is \$4,566, split:

- Current liabilities \$1,315
- Non-current liabilities \$3,251.

These figures will appear in the balance sheet as at the end of year 1.

Year 1's income statement will show:

- Finance charge on lease \$856
- Depreciation (one eighth of \$5,710) \$714

Example

Sum of the digits method

The same figures as before can be broken down as follows:

Total lease payments = \$8,000

Fair value of leased asset = \$5,710

Total finance charges = \$8,000 − 5,710 = \$2,290

This can be split by taking the "sum of the digits" of the payments. There are 4 payments, so we take 4+3+2+1 = 10.

The first payment includes 4/10 of the total finance charge, the second includes 3/10, the third 2/10 and the fourth and final payment includes 1/10. The resulting figures will be different from those calculated by the actuarial methid, but they will be a crude approximation to them.

Exam focus

You should only use the sum of the digits method if the examiner does not give you sufficient information to use the actuarial method.

Interest payments for year 1 = 4/10 of $2,290 = $916

Interest payments for year 2 = 3/10 of $2,290 = $687

This means that $2,000 – 916 = $1,084 will be repaid during year 1 and $2,000 – 687 = $1,313 will be repaid during year 2.

The asset will still be recorded at a cost of $5,710.

The balance sheet at the end of year 1 will show a liability totalling $5,710 – 1,084 = $4,626. This can be split:

- Current liabilities $1,313
- Non-current liabilities $3,313

Year 1's income statement will show:

- Finance charge on lease $916
- Depreciation $714

Disclosure

IAS 17 requires the following disclosures by lessees for finance leases:

- for each class of asset, the net carrying amount at the balance sheet date
- liability for finance leases split between current liabilities and
- non-current liabilities
- depreciation charge in the income statement
- finance charge in the income statement.

These disclosures are necessary, partly because the leased assets are treated as the lessee's for accounting purposes, but they are not actually the lessee's property. That could be significant if, for example, a potential lender was evaluating a loan applicant's capacity to offer security for a loan.

Operating leases

Operating leases are not capitalised in the same way as finance leases.

Most operating leases will be short term in nature and the lease payments will be written off as expenses as and when they are incurred.

If an operating lease spans more than one accounting period the rental charges should be charged to the income statement on a straight-line basis over the term of the lease, unless another systematic and rational basis is more appropriate.

This might arise if, for example, an office block was leased for three years while the lessee's own premises are being refurbished.

Any difference between amounts charged on operating leases and amounts paid will be treated as prepayments or accruals in the balance sheet.

For non-cancellable operating leases with a term of more than one year, commitments should be disclosed in summary form, giving the amounts and periods in which the payments will become due.

15

Substance over form

In this chapter

- Substance over form.
- IAS 18 Revenue.

SUBSTANCE OVER FORM

The requirement to reflect substance over form is laid down by IAS 1, the Framework and is implied in many of the developments in financial reporting.

Historically, companies have often preferred to report the legal form of transactions because that made it possible to enhance the impression created by the resulting financial statements.

For example, many years ago leasing was a popular type of financing because the accounting rules did not distinguish operating and finance leases. That meant that companies could lease assets instead of borrowing and thereby report lower liabilities, lower gearing and higher return on capital.

Key Point

The best starting point in dealing with matters of substance over form is to decide who bears the risks and rewards. That will normally provide the basis for deciding the best accounting treatment.

The concept of substance over form requires that the underlying economic substance be reported as opposed to the legal form. The implications of this have been developed in a number of specific cases.

Consignment inventory

In many businesses it is commonplace for inventory to remain the property of the manufacturer. For example, many vehicle manufacturers provide inventory on consignment to their distributors.

The terms on which consignment inventory is provided varies. In some cases it is clear that accepting delivery of inventory has the effect of passing the risks and rewards of ownership to the recipient.

Chapter 15

Sale and repurchase

Sometimes a manufacturer has to hold inventory for several years (e.g. a whisky distiller has to allow its product to mature). Such industries have developed a technique of borrowing against inventory by selling it to a bank, but giving the bank the option to sell the inventory back at a later date for a price equal to the original selling price plus interest. In such cases the inventory stays in the manufacturer's physical possession.

Historically, such arrangements were accounted for as sales. Nothing was reflected in the manufacturer's balance sheet. The fact that the bank had the right to sell the inventory back at some future date did not, in itself, create a legal liability during the life of this arrangement.

If it is clear that the inventory will be sold back to the manufacturer then it should be accounted for as a loan taken out at the time of the sale and the finance charges accrued over its duration.

IAS 18 Revenue

Definition

Revenue is the gross inflow of economic benefits during the period arising in the course of the ordinary activities of an entity.

Revenue is measured by the fair value of the consideration received or receivable.

Determining the point at which revenue has been earned can be complicated. The "risks and rewards" test described above will usually help decide when the revenue has been earned. It is not, however, too difficult to develop scenarios involving options to cancel or modify a transaction's terms which make the point at which real ownership passes.

16

Provisions, contingent liabilities and contingent assets

In this chapter

- Provisions.
- Contingent liabilities and contingent assets.
- Events after the balance sheet date.

Provisions

The accounting treatment of provisions is dealt with mainly by IAS 37 Provisions, contingent liabilities and contingent assets.

This is an area where there have been lots of abuses in the past. This means that the rules are complicated by the need to deal with a range of eventualities.

Definition

A **provision** is a liability of uncertain timing or amount.

IAS 37 requires that a provision should be recognised when:

- an enterprise has a present obligation (legal or constructive) as a result of a past event
- it is probable that an outflow of resources embodying economic benefits will be required to settle the obligation, and

- a reliable estimate can be made of the amount of the obligation.

Provisions cannot be recognised in the absence of a 'present obligation' because companies have, in the past, recognised provisions in order to smooth out reported earnings. Large provisions might be made in good years and then cancelled in bad years in order to create a steady trend in profits.

This is particularly true in the case of provisions for reorganisation. Before a provision can be made there has to be a detailed plan for the reorganisation and the company must have raised a valid expectation in those affected that it will take place (e.g. by issuing redundancy notices).

There is no formal definition of 'probable' but that is usually defined as "more likely than not", or even 50:50, in practice.

The amount recognised as a provision should be:

- a realistic estimate
- a prudent estimate of the expenditure needed to settle the obligation existing at the balance sheet date
- discounted back to net present value whenever the effect of this is material.

For each class of provision, an enterprise should disclose:

- opening and closing balance and movements during the year
- a brief description of the nature of the obligation and the expected timing of any resulting outflows, including an indication of the uncertainties about the amount and timing of outflows.

Contingent liabilities and contingent assets

IAS 37 also deals with this issue.

Definition

A **contingent liability** is:

- a possible obligation that arises from past events and whose existence will be confirmed only by the occurrence or non-occurrence of one or more uncertain future events not wholly within the control of the entity, or

- a present obligation that arises from past events but is not recognised because:

  - it is not probable that an outflow of resources embodying economic benefits will be required to settle the obligation, or

  - the amount of the obligation cannot be measured with sufficient reliability.

Contingent liabilities:

- should not be recognised in the balance sheet itself
- should be disclosed in a note unless the possibility of a transfer of economic benefits is remote.

Definition

A **contingent asset** is a possible asset that arises from past events and whose existence will be confirmed only by the occurrence or non-occurrence of one or more uncertain future events not wholly within the control of the enterprise.

Contingent assets should not generally be recognised, but if the possibility of inflows of economic benefits is probable, they should be disclosed.

Events after the balance sheet date

IAS 10 Events after the balance sheet date distinguishes between adjusting and non-adjusting events.

Definition

Adjusting events are events after the balance sheet date which provide additional evidence of conditions existing at the balance sheet date.

Adjusting events require the adjustment of amounts recognised in the financial statements. For example, the discovery that a major trade receivable should be written off as a bad debt should be reflected in the relevant income statement and balance sheet figures.

No further disclosure is necessary.

Non-adjusting events are events after the balance sheet date which concern conditions that arose after the balance sheet date.

Non-adjusting events should be disclosed by note if they are of such importance that non-disclosure would affect the ability of the users of the financial statements to make proper evaluations and decisions. For example, an uninsured loss arising from a fire that occurred after the balance sheet date.

The note should disclose the nature of the event and an estimate of the financial effect, or a statement that such an estimate cannot be made.

Proposed dividends

A major change in IAS 10 is that equity dividends proposed before but declared after the balance sheet date may no longer be included as liabilities at the balance sheet date.

The liability arises at the declaration date so they are non-adjusting events after the balance sheet date and must be disclosed by note as required by IAS 1.

Taxation

In this chapter

- Current tax.
- Sales tax.
- Deferred tax.
- Disclosure requirements.

Current tax

IAS 12 Income taxes lays down some basic requirements in respect of current tax:

- Current tax should be accounted for in the income statement unless the tax relates to an item that has been accounted for in equity.

- Tax rates used should be those that have been enacted by the balance sheet date. This will include those 'substantially enacted' by the balance sheet date.

- The figure for income tax on profits is an estimate of the amount that will be eventually paid and it appears in current liabilities in the balance sheet.

- Any under/over-provision is dealt with in the following year's tax charge.

Sales tax

Sales tax is known as Value Added Tax (VAT) in the UK and as general sales tax (GST) in some other countries.

Typically, it is an indirect tax on consumers that is collected for the authorities by traders.

Traders are not normally liable to pay sales tax and can reclaim any that they have paid on their inputs against the amounts collected for the government from their customers. Thus, revenues and costs are shown net of sales tax.

Deferred tax

Key Point

Deferred tax arises because profits can be recognised for accounting purposes in one period and for tax in another.

Some countries have two slightly different sets of rules for calculating profit for tax purposes as opposed to financial reporting.

Sometimes these differences are only temporary. That can mean that companies can recognise accounting profits in one period and be required to pay the related tax liability in a future period. There can also be occasions when they pay tax on profits that have not yet been recognised for financial reporting purposes.

Definition

Deferred tax is the estimated future tax consequences of transactions and events recognised in the financial statements of the current and previous periods.

Deferred tax arises because of **timing differences**. For example, in the UK a company would accrue interest receivable but would not pay tax on it until the interest is actually received.

The two main causes of timing differences are as follows:

- **Accelerated capital allowances** mean that non-current assets are written off very quickly after purchase. That means that companies can claim a lot of tax relief when non-current assets are new, but relatively little when the assets are older.

  In the short term more tax relief is claimed in the tax calculation than depreciation is charged in the income statement. That difference is cancelled in the longer term when depreciation catches up with the taxable capital allowances.

  Accelerated capital allowances mean that tax on profit is delayed, so there is a **deferred tax liability**.

- The tax treatment of **pension charges** mean that companies recognise an expense for tax purposes during employees' working lives, but cannot claim the associated tax relief until the pensions are actually paid after retirement.

Pension charges mean that companies incur expenses for accounting purposes but cannot claim the associated tax relief until much later.

Pension charges effectively mean that tax on profit is paid too soon, so there is a **deferred tax asset**.

IAS 12 requires that an enterprise should recognise a deferred tax liability or asset whenever the recovery or settlement of the carrying amount of an asset or liability would make future tax payments larger or smaller than they would be if such recovery or settlement were to have no tax consequences.

The deferred tax asset or liability is calculated by taking the cumulative timing differences outstanding at the year end and multiplying by the estimated tax rate that is likely to be in force when the difference reverses. This is usually taken to be the tax rate in force as at the year end.

Movements on the deferred tax asset or liability flow through the tax charge in the income statement.

Disclosure requirements

The main disclosures are:

- the tax expense (income) should be presented on the face of the income statement
- the major components of tax expense (income) should be disclosed separately in a note.

Current and deferred tax charged/credited to equity.

- An explanation of the relationship between tax expense (income) and accounting profit.
- A numerical reconciliation between tax expense (income) and the product of accounting profit multiplied by the

applicable tax rate(s), disclosing also the basis on which the applicable tax rate(s) is (are) computed.

18

Earnings per share

In this chapter

- IAS 33 Earnings per share.

IAS 33 Earnings per share

The earnings per share (EPS) has a standard devoted to its calculation because it is one component of the most important ratio used to measure a company's share price.

Stock market investors frequently refer to the price/earnings (P/E) ratio, which is calculated as:

Share price/EPS

A high P/E ratio indicates that the market is confident in the company's future.

In most cases, EPS is very easy to calculate:

Earnings/number of shares

IAS 33 requires that this be expressed in cents per share, calculated to one decimal place.

Earnings = group profit after tax, less minority interests and irredeemable preference share dividends.

Shares = weighted average number of ordinary shares outstanding during the period.

Most of the detail in IAS 33 deals with complications that might have the effect of distorting the EPS calculation.

Issue of shares at full market price

Earnings should be apportioned over the weighted average equity share capital (i.e. taking account of the date any new shares are issued during the year).

Bonus issue

A bonus issue does not provide any additional resources to the issuer. Its treatment is even simpler than that for an issue at full market price:

- The bonus shares are deemed to have been issued at the start of the year.

- Comparative figures are restated using the same higher share figure.

Rights issues

A rights issue can be best thought of as a combination of an issue at full market price, combined with a bonus issue.

The bonus element is calculated firstly by calculating the theoretical ex-rights price.

- For example, suppose that two new shares are to be issued at $1.50 each for every three previously held. The share price immediately prior to the rights being taken up was $2.20.

- In theory, every three shares held immediately before the issue will be worth $6.60. The issue will increase this to five shares worth a total of $6.60 + (2 × $1.50) = $9.60. Dividing by five will give a share price of $1.92.

The bonus element of the issue can be determined by the fraction:

Actual cum rights price / theoretical ex rights price.

- Suppose that our company had 300,000 shares in issue prior to the rights issue.

- The issue took place at the end of month three.

- The bonus element of the issue would increase the number of shares to 300,000 × 2.20/1.92 = 343,750.

- The full price element of the issue would increase the number of shares to 300,000 × 5/3 = 500,000.

- The comparative figures for last year's EPS will be calculated by dividing the earnings by 343,750.

- The weighed average shares in issue throughout the current year will be (343,750 × 3/12) + (500,000 × 9/12) = 460,938.

Diluted eps

The basic EPS figure can be confusing when the company's issued share capital is liable to change because of options, warrants, convertible shares, etc. Any of these could result in the company issuing fresh shares and "diluting" the EPS of existing shareholders.

Diluted EPS is calculated as:

$$\frac{\text{Earnings + notional extra earnings}}{\text{Number of shares + notional extra shares}}$$

Notional extra earnings arise when, for example, the conversion of a loan bond reduces interest charges while converting convertible preference shares will decrease preference dividend and increase earnings available for the equity shareholders.

Diluted EPS is a little more complicated when options or warrants grant the right to buy shares at a fixed price that is lower than the market price.

Exercising a warrant or option can be seen as purchasing some shares at fair value and receiving others as a bonus. Issuing shares at fair value does not dilute EPS, so only the bonus element is taken into account in restating the number of shares.

For example, suppose a company has 500,000 warrants outstanding that give the holders the right to buy one share for each at a price of $2.50. The stock market price of the shares was $3.00 at the year end. If all of the warrants were exercised at the year end then 500,000 x $2.50 = $1,250,000 would be raised. That is equivalent to selling $1,250,000 / $3.00 = 416,667 shares at fair value. The bonus element, which would be taken into account in calculating diluted EPS would be 500,000 – 416,667 = 83,333 shares.

Presentation and disclosure

Basic and Diluted EPS should be presented on the face of the income statement for each class of ordinary share.

Basic and Diluted EPS must be presented with equal prominence.

Basic and Diluted EPS should be presented even if the amounts are negative (i.e. a loss per share).

The following information should be disclosed for both basic and DEPS.

- The profit or loss used as numerators and a reconciliation of those amounts to the net profit or loss for the period.
- The weighted average number of ordinary shares used as the denominator and a reconciliation of the denominators to each.

19

Interpretation of financial statements

In this chapter

- Analysing financial statements.
- Interpreting current cost and current purchasing power accounts.
- IAS 24 Related party disclosures.

Analysing financial statements

Exam focus

Question 3 deals with the appraisal of performance. You are likely to be asked to interpret accounting information.

You should be familiar with the process of calculating accounting ratios from earlier stages. It is still possible that you will be able to earn marks for the calculation of ratios in this paper, but more marks will be available for the interpretation of the results.

Exam focus

There are probably more marks available for interpreting ratios in the exam than for their calculation.

Perspective

There is always a reason for interpreting accounting information. The purpose of the analysis will determine its focus and the depth. A bank manager thinking of extending a short-term overdraft facility might be interested in liquidity whereas a shareholder might be more interested in profitability.

Exam focus

Always read the question carefully and ensure that any position or perspective is taken into account in choosing and discussing ratios.

Sounding professional

The following hints and tips are based on many years of examining and marking for professional bodies.

- Know what each ratio means. If, for example, you know what the gross profit percentage is then you will not really need to memorise the formula. You will also find it easier to comment sensibly on the results.

- Look at the numbers before you calculate any ratios. If one company's turnover is three times the other's then it might have advantages in terms of economies of scale that could affect your analysis.

- Organise the ratios into groups and deal with them in a logical sequence. Profitability is usually more important than liquidity or gearing, so start with that. The return on capital employed is by far the most important profitability ratio. Good answers usually start with return on capital employed, then the secondary profitability ratios, then move on to liquidity and gearing.

Exam focus

Always read the requirements and context of the question. It is, however, quite common to find that return on capital employed is the

most logical starting point.

- Round sensibly. Percentages should be rounded off to whole numbers, as should days in the working capital ratios. The liquidity ratios can go to one decimal place. It looks unprofessional to provide meaningless accuracy.

- Don't exaggerate minor differences. If two companies have ratios that differ by a single percentage point then it is probably better to describe them as "similar" rather than building a case that one is better.

- If the numbers don't make sense then your calculations might be wrong. Remember that the accounts are meant to present a realistic case. If debtors are settling their balances within three days then you might have miscalculated the ratio.

- Justify your assertions. Don't say 'this company's ratio is higher and that makes it better'. Explain why the higher ratio is

- beneficial.

- Look for relationships between ratios. Try to demonstrate some commercial awareness. If, for example, a company has a healthy gross profit percentage and also spends a large proportion of its turnover on selling and distribution then it might be worth suggesting that the success in sales is partly due to investing in advertising.

Interpreting current cost and current purchasing power accounts

Historical cost accounting tends to report misleading and distorted results.

Asset values measured at cost less depreciation tend to undervalue non-current assets. This is becoming less of an issue with the tendency to reflect non-current assets at their fair values, but it is a problem that tends to persist.

Profit figures tend to be based on revenues that are compared with out of date (and generally understated costs).

For example, if a piece of inventory was purchased for $5 and sold some time later for $8 then the accounting system would record a profit of $3. If the inventory was then replaced at a cost of $7 then it could be argued that the company is only $1 better off if we allow for the effects of rising prices on the calculation of cost of sales.

The concepts of capital that we discussed briefly in chapter 2 offer alternative approaches to calculating profit and preparing balance sheets.

Current cost accounting

Current cost accounting (CCA) bases the figures in the income statement and the balance sheet on the cost of replacing assets consumed in generating profit and the replacement cost of assets as at the year end.

This has the effect of ensuring that the company cannot declare a profit unless it has maintained its productive capacity. For example, depreciation charges would allow for the replacement of non-current assets and the cost of sales calculation would say that the inventory sold for $8 had a replacement cost of $7 so the profit on that transaction would be reported at $1.

CCA accounts have limitations:

- Valuation of assets requires judgement, making comparisons harder. It is both difficult and expensive to prepare and audit CCA accounts.
- No account is taken of the effect of general inflation, only specific price changes. General inflation is a measure of the average increase in prices, but some items will rise by more than the rate of inflation, others by less and some prices might even fall over time.

- CCA profit does not necessarily show the real return to the shareholders. A shareholder might not even be particularly interested in whether the productive capacity of the business is maintained.

Current purchasing power

Current purchasing power (CPP) takes account of general inflation.

Historical figures are multiplied by indices that restate everything to year end $.

This has the effect of maintaining the financial capital of the business.

CPP accounts are easier to prepare because they use general index numbers that are provided by the government.

If a company reports a profit under CPP then that would mean that the company has taken the shareholders' capital and maintained and enhanced its value in monetary terms.

The resulting figures might not necessarily mean a great deal for decision making purposes. A CPP figure for a non-current asset might bear no relation to its fair value or replacement cost.

IAS 24 Related party disclosures

Two parties are considered to be related if one party has the ability to control the other party or exercise significant influence over the other party, or the parties under common control.

Where the reporting entity is controlled by another party then it must disclose:

- the related party relationship and the name of the party

- the ultimate controlling party, if different

- the amount of benefits paid to key management personnel should be disclosed.

If there have been transactions between related parties, the reporting entity should disclose:

- the nature of the related party relationships

- the types of transactions

- the details necessary for an understanding of the financial statements.

20

Cash flow statements

In this chapter

- IAS 7 Cash flow statements.
- Interpreting cash flow statements.

IAS 7 Cash flow statements

The performance appraisal in question 3 could include cash flow statements.

The cash flow statement provides an important insight into the ways in which the entity has created and applied cash during the period. The fact that a business generated profit during a period means that it has created wealth, but wealth is not necessarily reflected by cash. The fact that a business is liquid according to the balance sheet at the year end does not say a great deal about the cash movements that occurred during the year.

IAS 7 requires the provision of a cash flow statement that classifies cash flows into:

- operating activities
- investing activities
- financing activities.

The following pro-forma is useful for most questions:

Cash flows from operating activities

	$	$
Net profit before tax		X
Adjustments for:		
Interest expense		X
Depreciation		X
Profit on sale of non-current assets		X
Provisions		X
Government grants		X
Investment income		(X)
Operating profit before working capital changes		X
Inc/dec in inventories		(X)/X
Inc/dec in trade receivables		(X)/X
Inc/dec in trade payables		X/(X)
Cash generated from operations		X
Interest paid		(X)
Income taxes paid		(X)
Net cash from operating activities		X

Cash flows from investing activities:

	$	$
Purchases of property, plant and equipment	(X)	
Proceeds of sale of property, plant and equipment	X	
Interest received	X	
Dividends received	X	
Net cash used in investing activities		(X)

Cash flows from financing activities:

Proceeds from issue of shares	X	
Proceeds from long-term borrowings	X	
Payment of finance lease liabilities	(X)	
Dividends paid	(X)	
Net cash used in financing activities		(X)
Net increase in cash and cash equivalents		X
Cash and cash equivalents at beginning of period		X
Cash and cash equivalents at end of period		X

Analysis of cash and cash equivalents

	This year $	Last year $
Cash on hand and balances with banks	X	X
Short-term investments	X	X
Cash and cash equivalents	X	X

This approach to calculating cash generated from operations is known as the "indirect method". It starts with profit before tax from the income statement and:

- adjusts for interest to get back to profit from operations

- adjusts for non-cash items such as depreciation

- adjusts for increases and decreases in working capital.

It is possible to get the same result by means of the 'direct method', which states the actual cash flows associated with operations:

- cash received from customers
- cash paid to suppliers
- cash paid for expenses
- cash paid for wages and salaries.

The easiest way to determine these figures for the direct method is to produce a set of T accounts as workings.

For example, cash received from customers can be obtained by drafting the trade receivables account, entering the opening and closing balances from the balance sheets as at the beginning and end of the year and inserting all of the transactions recorded in the income statement (sales and bad debts).

Once the account has been drafted, it will be necessary to insert a balancing figure, which will be the cash received from customers.

This approach works equally well to the other operating figures.

The balancing figure approach can also be invaluable in obtaining figures for any of the other cash flows under other headings (transactions involving non-current assets, tax paid, etc).

Interpreting cash flow statements

The cash flow statement is a vital supplement to the other statements. Arguably, there is no point in a business existing if it cannot produce an adequate profit. However, cash can be more important in the short term because a business that runs short of cash could fail even if it has the capacity to generate profits and even return to a cash surplus in the longer term.

The cash flow statement provides another dimension to the liquidity position spelt out in the balance sheet.

Exam focus

You have to be careful not to make a hasty judgement about the net cash flow for the year.

It is not necessarily a good thing to generate a cash inflow or suffer a cash outflow. If a company is too liquid already then it would be better to invest in profit-making assets or to return the surplus funds to the shareholders as a dividend.

Similarly, raising cash is not an end in itself. It might be necessary to raise funds from borrowing, but the cash flow statement should be read in conjunction with the balance sheet to see what overall effect the changes during the year have had on the company's overall financial position.

You should also beware of short-term 'window-dressing' of the closing cash position. Delaying payments to suppliers and pressing customers for prompt payment can inflate cash balances (and improve some of the liquidity ratios) but the effects of this will disappear when the company returns to its normal practices after the balance sheet date.

Index